focus *grid, Marquis*

Grace Marquis

Author
    Grace Marquis

Coordinator of the *focus* series and Professor of Design
    Sarah McDowell

Special Thanks
    Geoff Newton for initiating the "*focus* series"
    Don Adelta for sharing the *focus* series concept

Photography
    Provided by Adobe Stock and Pixabay

Layout
    Typeset in Adobe Garamond Pro Regular and *Italic*
    File created with Adobe InDesign CC

Print
    Printing by Lulu Press Inc.
    Cover 100 lb. laminated cover stock. Text: 80l lb.

Edition Draft
    This edition was created in order to document the extent
    of research produced during the 2023 fall semester of the
    junior level BFA Graphic Design course at Ohio University.
    This was produced and distributed through Lulu Press, Inc.
    as a vehicle for additional research and discussion beyond
    course requirements.

978-1-304-89068-9

Table of Contents

Beginning

This is a project that started in the early fall of 2023. It began with the creation of 20 grids. I based these initial grids off of shapes found in the real world. Things like windows, fruit, and beads all formed inspiration for my work. Looking through the 20 grids, I needed to find one that I wanted to move forward with.

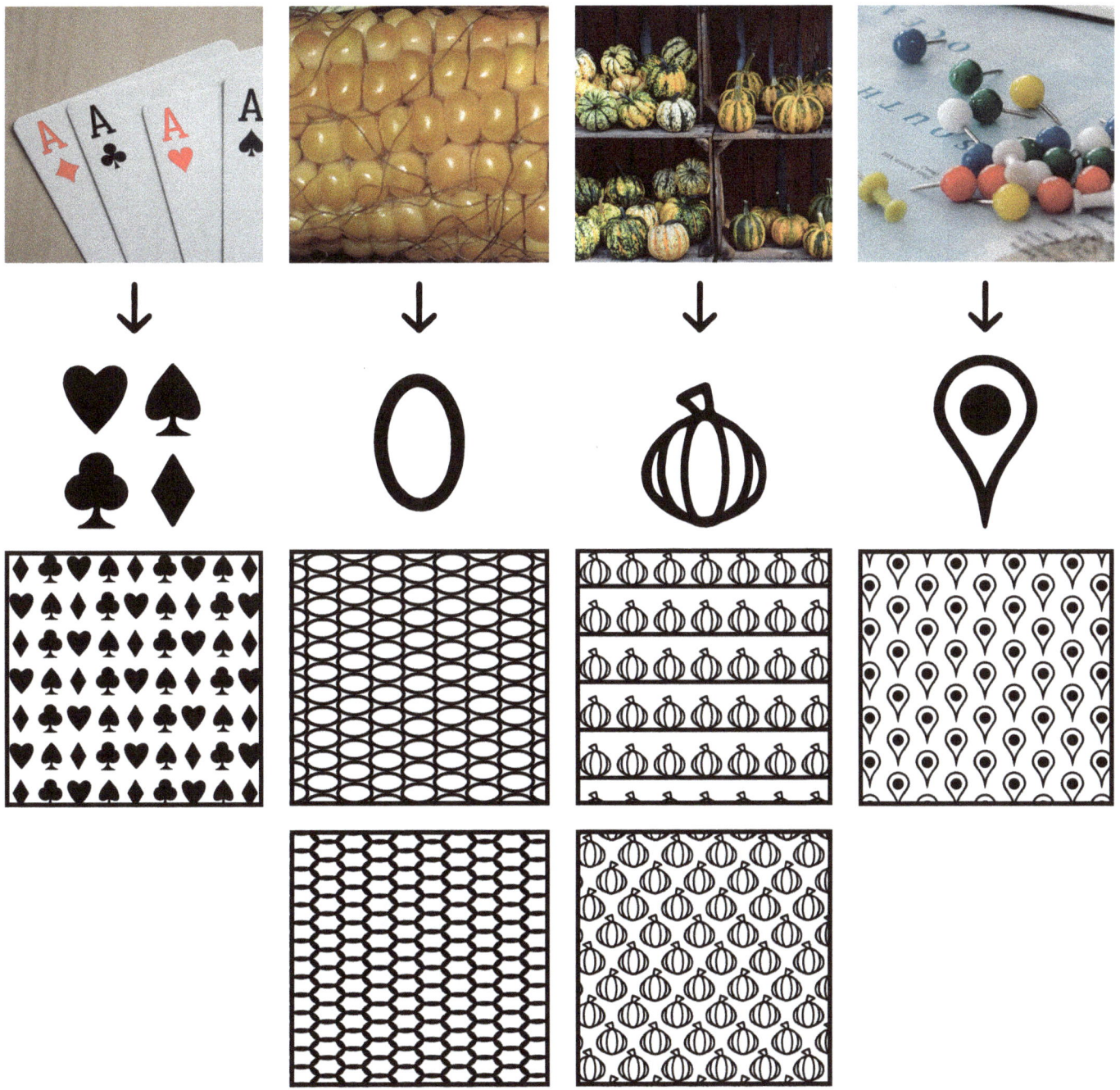

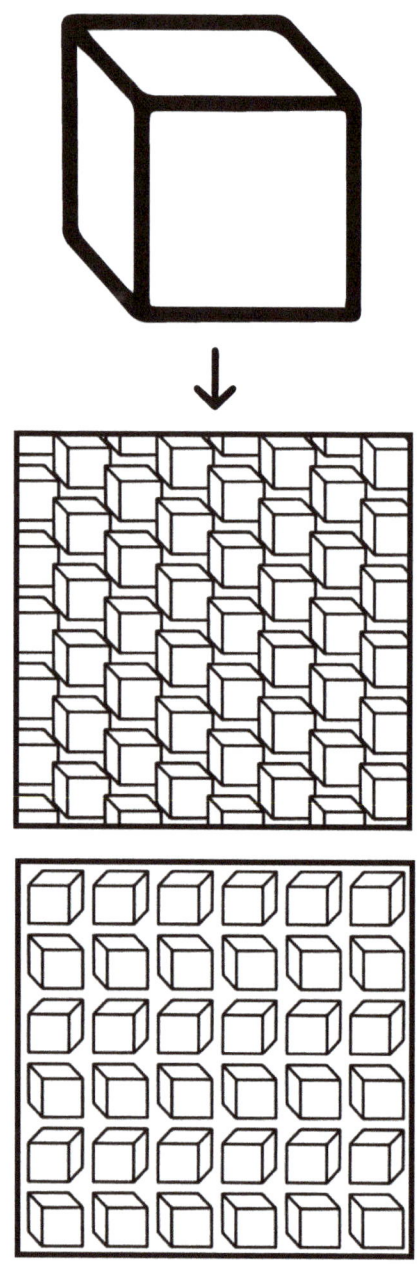

Taking it Further

The grid I decided to move forward with was inspired by a rug in my apartment. It has a design that features squares within squares. The translation of the rug into a grid format was one I found the most interesting, so I took it to the next step. Now I was able to create 120 iterations of the grid. This was done by moving features around, adding or subtracting elements, and manipulating scale.

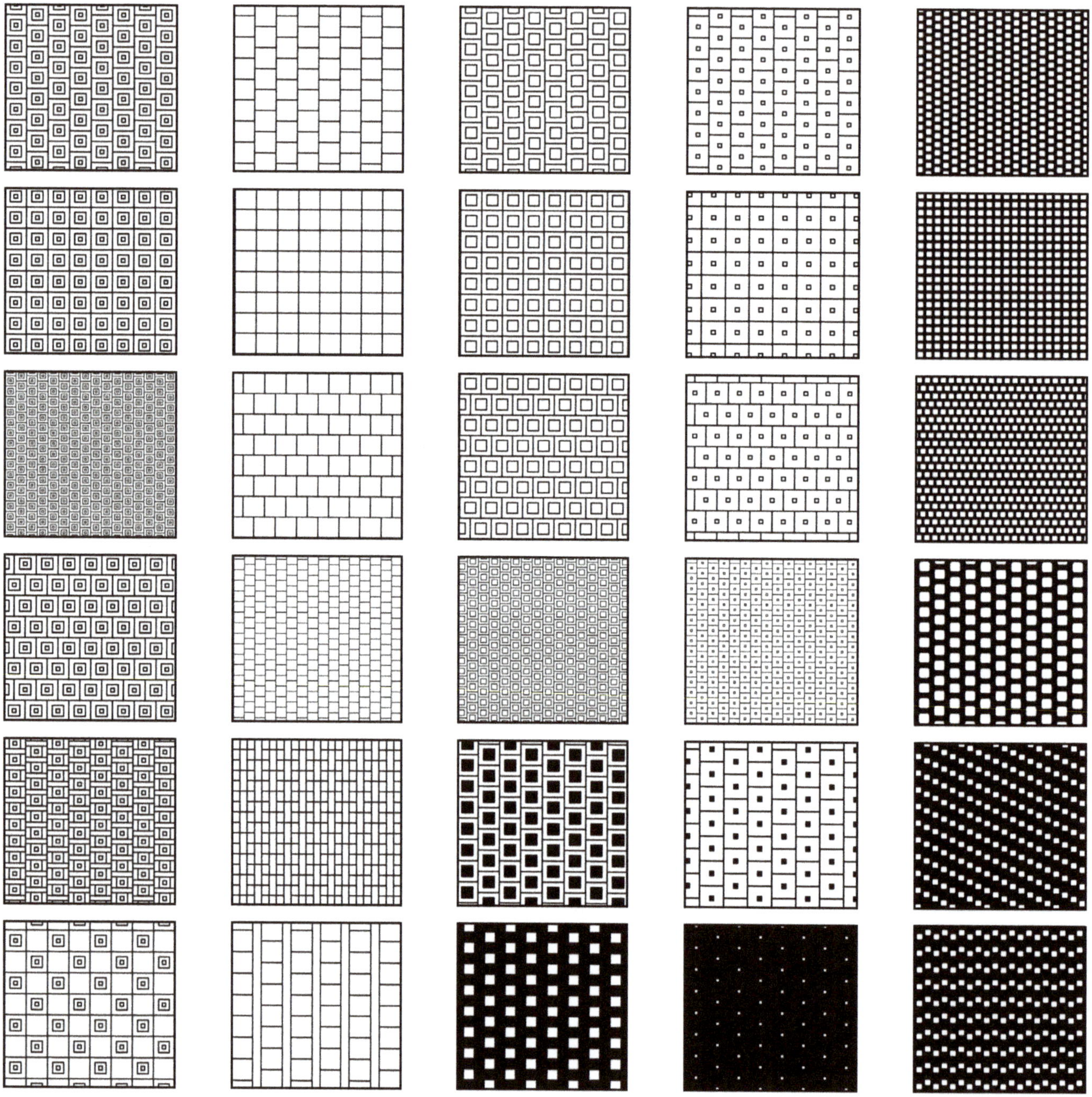

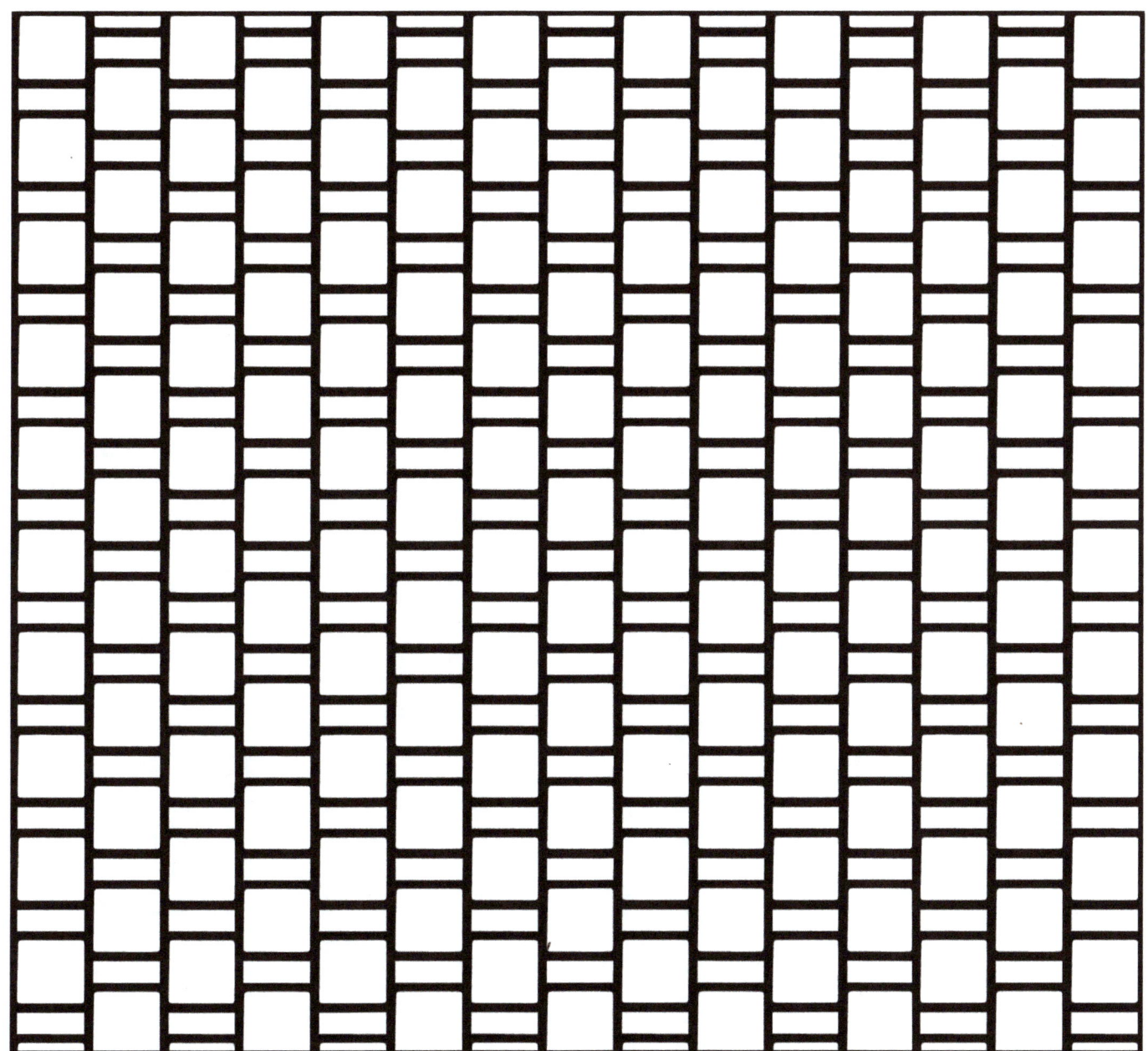

Associations

From these 120 grids, I began
searching for associations I
had with the shapes within
them. What was I reminded
of? I analyzed and made a note
of which ones reminded me
of what. From these analyses,
I would take one and apply
it to the physical world.

Application to the Physical World

The grid I chose to apply is one consisting of interconnecting squares. It reminded me of a decorative kitchen dish cloth, so I began transforming it into that. After creating three cloths, I wanted to do more. I started thinking about ways to apply the grid to other home decor. I applied it to various surfaces. The ones I believe work the strongest feature the grid on window curtains and on a large rug.

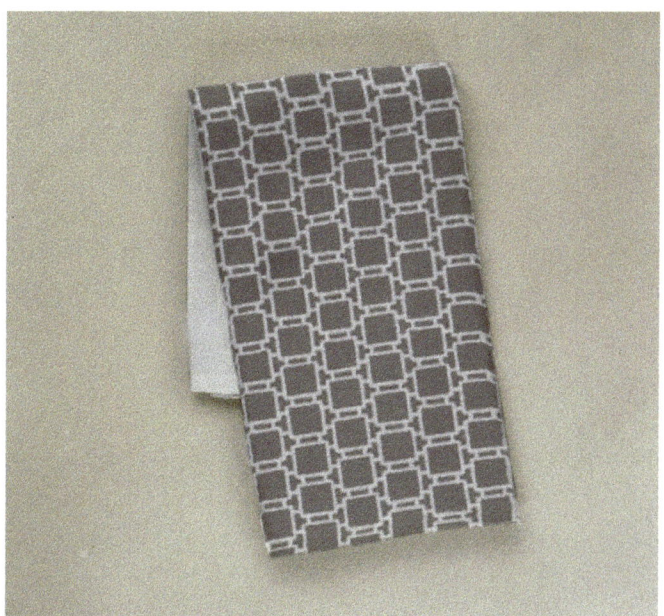